AMERICA'S NATIONAL PARKS

A Photographic Journey

TEXT: **James P. Delgado**

CAPTIONS: **Nicola Dent**

DESIGN: **Teddy Hartshorn**

PRODUCTION: **Ruth Arthur, Sally Connolly**

DIRECTOR OF PRODUCTION: **Gerald Hughes**

PICTURE SOURCES: **Colour Library Books Ltd., Anne B. Keiser,
Brandenburg Stock, Will Goddard,
Kent and Donna Dannen**

CLB 2882
© 1992 Colour Library Books Ltd., Godalming, Surrey, England.
All rights reserved.
This 1992 edition published by Crescent Books,
distributed by Outlet Book Company, Inc., a Random House Company,
40 Engelhard Avenue, Avenel, New Jersey 07001.
Printed and bound in Malaysia
Color separations by Scantrans Pte Ltd., Singapore.
ISBN 0 517 07257 2
8 7 6 5 4 3 2 1

AMERICA'S NATIONAL PARKS

A Photographic Journey

Text by
JAMES P. DELGADO

CRESCENT BOOKS
NEW YORK • AVENEL, NEW JERSEY

The concept of national parks was born in the United States. From America the idea spread throughout the world, and now more than a hundred nations contain national parks or preserves. The national park system of the United States is composed of 355 units. Only fifty of these units are actual "national parks," while the rest fall under twenty-two further designations, including national monuments, national historic sites, national memorials, national seashores, national preserves, and national recreation areas, among others. Each is a unit or area administered by the National Park Service for "park, monument, historic, parkway, recreational, or other purposes," fitting Congress' 1970 definition of the national park system.

Seventy-nine national monuments each preserve at least one nationally significant resource. They are usually smaller than national parks and do not possess their diversity. National historical parks and other cultural parks such as national battlefields, national military parks, national historic sites, and national memorials, compose about half of the national park system. These areas protect, preserve and interpret places associated with events, activities and people important in American history. They range from prehistoric Indian cultures to Civil War battlefields, from presidential sites to areas closely connected with prominent Americans, such as Thomas Edison, the Wright brothers, Booker T. Washington, Clara Barton and Martin Luther King, Jr.

National parks generally cover large tracts of land and contain a variety of resources – natural, cultural, recreational and scenic – and encompass sufficient land or water to ensure their protection. They are "inviolable sanctuaries" set aside in the interest of the people to preserve the exceptional quality of the natural world, American history, and scenery.

Forty-nine states, the District of Columbia, Guam, Puerto Rico, American Samoa, Saipan, and the Virgin Islands host the national park system. Some states contain more parks than others; Alaska, with more than fifty million acres of park lands, has the majority of total land area – thirteen percent of the state – in the system. The American city with the greatest park presence is Washington, D.C., hosting a unique park system that has been managed by the Federal government since 1791. Nearly every public park, square and monument in the District is included in the National Capital Region of the National Park Service.

The concept of national parks was born of the nationalistic pride of young America in the early nineteenth century, as the vastness and wonder of the continent was opened to public scrutiny, particularly after the Lewis and Clark expedition offered Euro-Americans the first inkling of what the western portion of the continent had to offer. Explorers, fur traders, and mountain men venturing into the wilderness were awed and inspired by what they saw. Artist George Catlin, who witnessed the passing of the frontier in 1832 while at Fort Pierre in what is now South Dakota, called for "a nation's park, containing man and beast, in all the wild and freshness of their nature's beauty!" Catlin's call for preservation was not answered. Sadly, the Mandan Indians Catlin painted were virtually exterminated by disease. The tragedy of America's failure to answer George Catlin's call was also reflected in time by the fencing in of the prairie, the mass killing of the buffalo, and the construction of the railroad, acts that ended the frontier as Catlin had seen it. Instead of a "beautiful and thrilling specimen" of the "nation's park" that would be a legacy "for America to preserve and hold up to the view of her refined citizens and the world, in future ages," this was the sad reality of Catlin's unheard plea.

Historian Alfred Runte traces the beginning of the movement to establish national parks to the inferiority nineteenth-century Americans felt in relation to Europe and its many centuries of human history. Not possessing the wonders of the ancient world or European civilization, Americans drew inspiration from the magnificent natural wonders of the New World. The first great natural attraction of North America to become well known was Niagara Falls. But the popularity of the falls proved its undoing, as vulgar developments and commercialization rapidly dominated the banks of the Niagara after 1830. The apparent American trend of treating natural wonders shabbily was decried by foreign visitors. Sir Richard Henry Bonny-castle, writing in 1849, found evidence in Niagara Falls' fate that "patriotism, taste, and self esteem are not the leading feature in the character of the inhabitants of this part of the world." As Runte noted, these criticisms hit a responsive chord in a nation that lacked an established past and had not yet notably expressed itself in art, architecture and literature, yet which saw in North American natural wonders "proof of national greatness."

The renewed push West in the aftermath of the Mexican War, the annexation of Pacific and Southwest territories, the California Gold Rush, and post-Civil War interest in the far western territories brought new discoveries of natural and scenic wonders. These discoveries, a counterpart to European cultural landmarks, provided a fresh challenge to hold them sacred and inviolate from development and com-mercialization. The essays of journalists helped focus attention on the newly found wonders. However, as Samuel Bowles wrote in 1865, "The Yosemite! As well interpret God in thirty-nine articles as portray it to you by word of mouth or pen." The growing interest in America's great scenery and natural wonders coincided with the growth of landscape painting in the United States and Europe, where artists evoked "the physical conditions" of the world on expansive canvases.

The success of this school of art profoundly affected public opinion. A case in point is the painting of the falls of the Niagara by Frederic Edwin Church, which elevated Church to the status of most famous American painter of the late nineteenth century. Church captured the essential quality of the place and created a dramatic scene that enveloped the viewer. "The spectator stands looking directly upon the troubled waters, flowing at the very base line of the canvas ... the eye naturally travels with the current until it reaches the brink of the invisible abyss into which the water tumbles ..." according to art historian David Huntington. The large landscape paintings of the wilderness by Thomas Moran and Albert Bierstadt similarly captured the "sheer monumentalism" of the Yosemite Valley and Yellowstone, engendering support for the preservation of these wonders by providing the visual component of the cultural nationalism that manifested itself in the drive for national parks.

Historian Roderick Nash points to the United States' unique experience with nature, its democratic ideals, vast public lands and affluent society as primary influences on the national park idea. Public attitudes changed about nature, which was slowly being viewed by some Americans as worthy of wonder and enhancing the quality of life, rather than something to be tamed and exploited. The new attitude toward nature joined with national insecurity and cultural nationalism to spawn the national parks.

Congressional establishment of a national

reservation at Arkansas' Hot Springs in 1832 that subsequently entered the national park system did not embody the goals later defined for a national park. The act stemmed from the need to protect the purportedly healing waters for public benefit through medicinal spa development, not for conservation. The first Federal effort to create a natural park was the Congressional protection of California's Yosemite Valley. The valley, discovered by settlers in 1851, was by the end of the decade eagerly sought by people motivated by "a spirit of romance; the love of the grand and beautiful in scenery ... the want of recreation, or the necessity of a restoration and recuperation of an over-tasked physical or mental organization, or both ..." in the words of *Hutchings California Magazine* in October, 1859. Yosemite Valley fulfilled the national requirement that such a park be monumental, awe-inspiring, and matchless in wonder to European marvels. "The first view of this convulsion-rent valley, with its perpendicular mountain cliffs, deep gorges, and awful chasms, spread out before us like a mysterious scroll, took away the power of thinking, much less of clothing thoughts with suitable language ...." The valley inspired one writer to ask, "Did mortal eyes ever behold such a scene in any other land?"

The need to preserve the scenic wonder of the Yosemite Valley and the nearby Sierra redwoods inspired California Senator John Conness to author a bill in early 1864. The bill, which was signed into law by President Abraham Lincoln on June 30, 1864, passed control of the valley, to which title was inalienable, to the State of California for "public use, resort, and recreation." Thus, in fact if not in name, the first national park was born.

The first national park in name was created in 1872 when 3,300,000-acre Yellowstone National Park, the world's foremost, was established by Congress. Significant precedents were established in the creation of the park. The first was the assertion that parks were to be created with lands worthless for any purpose except tourism born out of the desire to view magnificent wonders. The second was the involvement of

the Northern Pacific Railroad, which derived from the park's creation a financial boon through the transportation of tourists. Thus was born a pragmatic, symbiotic relationship between the transportation industry and park supporters. This scenario repeated itself time and again in the creation of other national parks.

Most important, however, was the beginning of a practice that was described by the president of the American Civic Association in 1916 as "some great man's thought of service to his fellow citizens. These parks did not just happen; they came about because earnest men and women became violently excited at the possibility of these great assets passing from public control .... These great parks are ... a sheer expression of democracy." The "separation of these lands from the public domain, to be held for the public, instead of being opened to private settlement" resulted in parks that served a higher interest as "the Nation's pleasure grounds and the Nation's restoring places, recreation grounds ...," with recreation meaning re-creation of the human spirit in the world of the industrial age. Yet that ugly world intruded, in the form of persistent battles to ensure that parks, however noble, did not interfere with the American preoccupation with making a dollar.

The majority of national parks established in the last decades of the nineteenth century and the early twentieth century, as well as the later monuments, were so-called "worthless lands," such as Glacier, Crater Lake, and Mount Rainier national parks. Compromises were necessary to create parks where worthlessness was not completely established, hence mining, hunting, and reclamation was allowed to continue in some parks. Thus strip mining would later be allowed in Death Valley National Monument, while hunting and other exploitation occured in many different areas, establishing a double standard that allowed for economic profit through mining, hunting, and logging of supposedly inviolable lands "in the national interest," while not allowing for private ownership and development of the same.

The continued opening of the West, meanwhile, led to the discovery and exploitation of the remnants of prehistoric civilizations in the Southwest. Now, through archaeology, the nation could gain an ancient past, making, as historian Runte notes, the cliff dwellings "suffice for the absence of Greek and Roman ruins in the New World." Therefore, the threat of destruction of the cliff dwellings and other ruins, and the dissolution of this cultural patrimony through souvenir hunting and vandalism, inspired the next push for national parks. Iowa Congressman John F. Lacey, seeking to preserve "American antiquities" as represented by "all objects of historical and cultural interest that are situated upon the lands owned or controlled by the Government ..." authored the bill. Signed into law in 1906, the Antiquities Act established the means for Presidential proclamation of national monuments.

Theodore Roosevelt, concluding that the inclusion of the term "scientific" in the legislation meant that geological features could be designated as national monuments, underscored this broad interpretation with his first proclamation of a national monument on September 24, 1906. That first monument was Devil's Tower, Wyoming, an 865-foot-high columnar rock remaining from a volcanic intrusion. Three more monuments quickly followed: El Morro, New Mexico's "inscription rock," carvings on which dated from antiquity to seventeenth-century Spanish explorers and nineteenth-century American emigrants and settlers, the Petrified Forest of Arizona, and Montezuma Castle, in Arizona, one of the best preserved cliff dwellings in the United States. Another famous Roosevelt proclamation was the establishment of Grand Canyon National Monument, on January 11, 1908; yet another was his sweeping declaration of a 600,000-acre monument on Washington's Olympic Peninsula on March 3, 1909.

Roosevelt's willingness to apply broadly the Antiquities Act through eighteen national monument proclamations provided a large number of areas that would someday become part of the national park system: twenty-seven monuments contributing to twenty-four future national parks. The Antiquities Act also led to

the largest category ultimately administered by the National Park Service, the seventy-nine national monuments. In 1916, when only one "cultural" national park, Mesa Verde, existed, the monuments also contributed a substantial cultural component to the future system. Nearly a fourth of the national park system traces its roots to the Antiquities Act.

By 1916, the year the National Park Service was created, the national park system encompassed 4,750,000 acres in fourteen parks, which included many of the "gems": Yellowstone, Yosemite, Grand Canyon, Glacier, Mount Rainier, Crater Lake, Mesa Verde, and Rocky Mountain. A fifteenth park had been established in 1875 on Mackinac Island, but within twenty years had been heavily logged and developed; in 1895, Mackinac Island National Park had been ceded to the State of Michigan. Moreover, twenty-one national monuments, as well as the Arkansas Hot Springs Reservation and, after its 1918 redesignation as a monument, the Casa Grande Ruin Reservation in Arizona, were combined in 1916 to form a thirty-eight-area National Park System.

The creation of the National Park Service was the first successful step in an effort to establish a central federal bureau responsible for the national parks, monuments, and other natural wonders and cultural sites. This effort would not be concluded until 1933, when monuments and other sites under the jurisdiction of the War and Agriculture departments were added to the national park system. Coupled with a desire to manage these diverse areas uniformly was the strong conviction of many conservationists that the federal government was slowly destroying the parks by allowing development – forest harvesting, reclamation, road building, and mining – to continue on park lands. The threat to the national parks was underscored by the fierce battles over the construction of the Hetch Hetchy Reservoir in Yosemite National Park.

The City and County of San Francisco faced a serious lack of fresh water shortly after the city boomed into a major metropolis following the California gold discovery in 1848. Water from beyond the city limits was tapped by means of an elevated redwood flume in 1858, when San Francisco's first permanent water system was constructed. As the city grew, this system was augmented, then replaced by a series of reservoirs, flumes and pipes south of San Francisco in nearby San Mateo County in the 1860s and '70s. The precedent of going far afield for water was reinforced at the century's end, when continued growth led city engineers to seek a new water supply. The logical source, in San Francisco politicians' eyes, was the Hetch Hetchy Valley in Yosemite National Park. Considered an unspoiled rival to the now crowded Yosemite Valley, the Hetch Hetchy was a natural wonder worthy of national park protection, which it supposedly enjoyed. Against this high standard, however, were pitted the needs of San Francisco. The city argued that a flooded Hetch Hetchy Valley would provide pure water for a million people and generate inexpensive hydroelectric power. Conservationists argued that an incomparable natural treasure would be forever lost.

The battle over the Hetch Hetchy raged for more than a decade, with San Francisco kicking it off in 1901. Initially denied in 1903, the city's request was approved by Secretary of the Interior James A. Garfield in 1908. The battle commenced in earnest. At stake lay, as Alfred Runte termed it, not the fringes of a park, but rather its very heart, as well as the national park idea. If the Hetch Hetchy Valley could not be protected from exploitation, then no other park, no other resource, was inviolate. But Congress upheld Garfield's decision in 1913 despite intense lobbying by conservationists.

On December 19, 1913, President Woodrow Wilson signed the enabling legislation for the city's use of the valley, saying, "It seems to serve the pressing public needs of the region concerned better than they could be served in any other way, and yet does not impair the usefulness or materially detract from the beauty of the public domain." Work began in 1914 to build a 430-foot high dam across the gorge. The completed O'Shaughnessy Dam blocked the Tuolumne River and flooded the valley in 1923;

a 149-mile-long aqueduct finished in 1934 carried the water to San Francisco. Thus ended, in defeat, the first major national battle for a national park. Yet as historian Nash observed, the importance of the fight was that it was national – for the first time, divergent groups and interests had joined together and coalesced the national park idea into a firm stand that led to a concerted push resulting in the 1916 organic act of the National Park Service.

Woodrow Wilson, whose signature doomed the Hetch Hetchy Valley, also penned into law the act establishing the National Park Service, in part the result of his earlier action, on August 25, 1916. Significant was the charge to the new bureau to leave the parks "unimpaired for the enjoyment of future generations." The man in charge of the new bureau was Stephen T. Mather. Mather, a wealthy borax mining magnate, was so angered by the mismanagement of Yosemite during a 1914 vacation that he wrote to Secretary of the Interior Franklin Lane to complain. Lane, sagely noting Mather's experience, wealth, and drive, replied that Mather could come to Washington and run the parks himself. Stephen Mather took the Secretary up on his offer. Joined by Interior Department lawyer Horace Albright, who served as his assistant, Mather helped ensure the passage of the National Park Service bill. Mather, as first director of the National Park Service, and his successor, Albright, brought into existence many of the features that characterize the National Park Service today – information centers, interpretive programs, uniformed rangers, concessionaires in the parks, and professional management of natural and cultural resources.

Under Mather and Albright's vision, the parks boomed in popularity, in large part due to a pragmatic marriage of opportunity with the railroads, who saw economic gain in promoting rail travel to the parks. Increased visitation meant more public support, and Mather and Albright staunchly backed railroad tourism. The new national park system boomed under their leadership; between 1916 and 1933 the system doubled in size; twelve new parks were created, six from previously proclaimed national monuments, while twelve new national monuments were declared. These years saw the introduction of more of the flagship parks: Mount McKinley (now part of Denali National Park); Sieur de Monts, now Acadia; Great Smoky Mountains; Mammoth Cave; Isle Royale; Zion; Badlands; Grand Teton; Glacier Bay and Bryce Canyon. Originally confined to the West, by 1933 the formerly regional national park system became national in scope.

Between 1916 and 1933 the National Park Service acquired several cultural sites, including some prehistoric archaeological sites and historical areas associated with the colonial period and the Revolutionary War. These additions were prescient – as National Park Service historian Barry Mackintosh notes, they launched the Service on a new course in the preservation of historic sites that greatly influenced the later growth and development of the national park system. The trend was confirmed in a reorganization of the executive branch of the federal government in 1933. Franklin Delano Roosevelt, under the authority of a bill approved by his predecessor Herbert Hoover, signed executive orders on June 10 and July 28, 1933. These transferred to the National Park Service the national military parks and cemeteries administered by the War Department, the national monuments of the Agriculture Department, and the national capital parks in the District of Columbia previously under the jurisdiction of an independent office reporting to the President. The national park system grew by ten new parks and fifty historical areas. The inclusion of these parks and memorials changed the definition of the national park system, which now included sites and areas not previously included in a park concept founded on the principles of preserving monumental natural wonders and prehistoric ruins. The National Park Service benefited through the redefinition of its purpose by an enhanced stature and influence: it was now responsible for nearly every federally owned parkland, monument and memorial.

Among the more intriguing and challenging tasks that resulted from the 1933 reorganization was the National Park Service's new duty to maintain what social historian Edward Tabor Linenthal has termed "reservoirs of sacred power" – American battlefields hallowed by the spilling of blood. The most common, and the most indicative of the tragedy of war to most, were the Civil War battlegrounds and their fields of dead soldiers buried row on row. In the immediate aftermath of battle, the setting aside of land, usually for the burial of the fallen, was a matter of national pride. Abraham Lincoln, speaking at the dedication of a portion of the bloody fields of Gettysburg, the most famous of these occasions, transformed, in the words of the park guidebook, that battlefield "from a scene of carnage into a symbol, giving meaning to the sacrifice of the dead and inspiration to the living."

There are now thirty-five battlefields and battlegrounds preserved in the national park system. Most of them are Civil War sites – the so-called "cannonball circuit" – with names famous in the annals of the war: Antietam, Manassas, Vicksburg, Fort Sumter and Shiloh – to name but a few. Many of these symbols of sacrifice, perseverance and dedication to a cause, were administered in the late nineteenth century and the first decades of the twentieth century by the War Department, the states, or other entities. Other battlefields and battlegrounds in the system commemorate different conflicts. Palo Alto Battlefield in Texas preserves the site on which the opening moves of the largely forgotten Mexican War of 1846-1848 were made. The more famous Revolutionary War sites include Minute Man National Historical Park in Concord, Massachusetts, where "the shot heard round the world" heralded the revolution, and Yorktown, part of Colonial National Historical Park and the place where Cornwallis' surrender signaled the end of British domination.

Some sites enshrine controversial but important conflicts. Custer Battlefield, where the Battle of the Little Bighorn occurred on June 25, 1876, marks not only the site of a defeat notorious for the annihilation of every last white man, but the Pyrrhic victory of the Sioux and

Cheyenne, who vanquished Custer in their struggle to preserve a way of life being swept away by the frontier's push West. It is grimly ironic that this site also commemorates the tragedy of the cultural destruction of the American Indians—in large part the reason why George Catlin called for a "nation's park" here in 1832.

Another momentous defeat, also a site in the national park system, is of a more recent date. On the morning of December 7, 1941, Japanese carrier-based aircraft attacked the United States Pacific Fleet at anchor in Pearl Harbor. The attack propelled the United States into the Second World War with the slogan "Remember Pearl Harbor!" The blasted, burning masts of the battleship *Arizona*, emblazoned against a smoke-filled sky, was one of the starker images of the "day of infamy." An armor-piercing shell penetrating the forward decks set off the battleship's magazines and fuel bunkers, nearly breaking the ship in half and sinking it in a cataclysmic explosion that showered the harbor with debris and bodies. Too badly damaged to be raised, the ship was left as a war grave in the oil-stained waters of Pearl Harbor. In 1966, an arched memorial was built to straddle the sunken hulk, by then rusted and coated with marine growth and still leaking oil from its bunkers. The USS *Arizona Memorial*, now jointly managed by the National Park Service and the U.S. Navy, is the most significant World War II site in the United States. Indelibly impressed into the national memory, the Pearl Harbor attack is symbolized by the *Arizona Memorial*, visited by millions every year who confront the face of war through a battleship whose wounds still bleed after half a century.

Other memorials in the national park system celebrate human achievement. Nestled in the sand dunes of North Carolina's Outer Banks on Bodie Island, the Wright Brothers National Memorial reflects the momentous aeronautic accomplishment of Orville and Wilbur Wright. Here at Kill Devil Hills on December 17, 1903, the Wrights made the first sustained flight in a heavier-than-air machine. Another memorial, Mount Rushmore, made history solely through

its creation. Blasted and hammered, then "bumped" to create a smooth finish in granite, the heads of four American presidents were hewn into the Black Hills of South Dakota to create a shrine of democracy. Conceived by South Dakota historian Doane Robinson and promoted by South Dakota politicians, the memorial was the life achievement of John Gutzon de la Mothe Borglum, who first studied the proposal in 1924. Established as a National Memorial on August 10, 1927, Mount Rushmore was laboriously transformed into a monumental sculpture over the next fourteen years. The heads of George Washington, Thomas Jefferson, Abraham Lincoln and Theodore Roosevelt symbolize the birth and trials of the first 150 years of the United States as well as individually representing the ideals of the Union.

One of the best-known symbols of the nation is also part of the national park system. The Statue of Liberty recently celebrated a centennial and a restoration that brought the attention of the world once again to this national monument, which stands at the historic point of entry to America. A gift from the people of France to the United States, the statue is a potent symbol of the human embodiment of liberty. The work of sculptor Auguste Bartholdi and engineer Gustave Eiffel, the statue and its wrought-iron support pylon were placed on a monumental base erected on Bedloe's, now Liberty Island. The completed statue, dedicated on October 28, 1886, came to represent not only political liberty, but freedom and the hope of a new life in America for generations of immigrants.

Other memorials commemorate various presidents. Washington, D.C. is home to dozens of memorial statues, squares, circles and monuments, among the most notable being the Jefferson Memorial (completed in 1943), the Washington Monument (1885) and the Lincoln Memorial (1922). Across the Potomac is the memorial to a later president, the Lyndon Baines Johnson Memorial Grove in Virginia. Theodore Roosevelt Island, also on the Potomac, is a living memorial to that president in the District of Columbia. In New York, General Grant National Memorial, more popularly known as "Grant's

Tomb," commemorates the life and career of Ulysses S. Grant, and covers a crypt that contains the remains of Grant and his wife. Another great American, Confederate General Robert E. Lee, is honored by the Custis-Lee Mansion in Arlington Cemetery. Lee's onetime home was designated a national memorial in 1972. Another memorial, to explorer Juan Rodriguez Cabrillo, the "discoverer" of California, is now a national monument in San Diego.

Four areas that symbolize international amity are also included in the National Park System. Roosevelt Campobello International Park, jointly owned and managed by Canada and the United States through an international commission, lies north of Lubec, Maine, on the Canadian shores of Passamaquoddy Bay. The summer home of Franklin Delano Roosevelt until he was stricken with polio in 1921, Campobello is now the only international unit of the park system and a monument to an extraordinary man respected not only by the citizens of the two countries, but the world. St. Croix Island International Historic Site, on the St. Croix River, the boundary between Maine and New Brunswick, Canada, marks the site of a French settlement of 1604. Another park with strong links to Canada is Perry's Victory and International Peace Memorial at Put-in-Bay, Ohio. The 352-foot-tall Doric column, surmounted by an eleven-ton bronze urn, memorializes not only the epic naval victory of Oliver Hazard Perry over a superior force at the Battle of Lake Erie on September 10, 1812, but also lasting peace between the United States and Canada that ensued, in part due to Perry's magnanimous treatment of the vanquished. The third international park, Chamizal National Memorial, lies on a portion of Cordova Island on the Rio Grande River, the border between the United States and Mexico. The park marks the peaceful 1963 settlement of a ninety-nine-year boundary dispute. A cultural pavilion and an auditorium showcasing the musical and dramatic culture of both nations are matched by a Mexican sister park across the river in Cuidad Juarez.

Preserving and interpreting the American past has been an aspect of the national park experience since the passage of the Antiquities Act of 1906 and the establishment of national monuments and parks to protect prehistoric ruins. Prehistoric sites include the well-known cliff dwellings of the Southwest parks and monuments: Canyon de Chelly, Bandelier, Mesa Verde, and Chaco Canyon are a few. Other sites include Ocmulgee in Macon, Georgia, which epitomizes the Indian mound-builder civilization of the American Southeast. Pu'uhonua o Honaunau National Historical Park, on the island of Hawaii, preserves a sacred city of refuge that contains prehistoric royal house sites, fishponds and coconut groves. In Alaska, Cape Krusenstern National Monument encompasses Inuit archaeological sites that date as far back as 4,000 years, along a progression of 114 beach ridges that in themselves document the tremendous geological changes near the now sunken prehistoric gateway from Asia into America. Russell Cave National Monument in Alabama preserves an almost continuous archaeological record of human habitation from 7000 B.C. to A.D. 1650.

European exploration and settlement are also represented in a series of parks and monuments. Fort Raleigh National Historic Site marks the site of Sir Walter Raleigh's "lost colony" of 1585, while further north in Virginia, Colonial National Historical Park incorporates Jamestown, the first permanent English settlement in the Americas. In Arizona, the Coronado National Memorial at Hereford commemorates Hispanic exploration near the site where Francisco Vázquez de Coronado entered the territory during his epic expedition of 1540-1542. A similiar site, the De Soto National Memorial at Bradenton, Florida, marks the 1539 landing and first extensive organized exploration of the southern United States by Europeans led by Hernan de Soto. Four Spanish missions in Texas along the San Antonio River – San Jose y San Miguel de Aguayo, Concepcion, San Francisco de la Espada, and San Juan Capistrano – compose San Antonio Missions National Historical Park, while Tumacacori National Monument preserves another mission, San Jose de Tumacacori, in Arizona.

Other aspects of the American cultural experience have been preserved in units of the national park system. The founding principles of the nation are memorialized at Independence National Historical Park in Philadelphia, which preserves the buildings and sites where the Continental Congress met during the American Revolution, the Declaration of Independence and the Constitution were drafted and where Congress and the Supreme Court were convened for ten years prior to the establishment of the permanent national capital in the District of Columbia. Another national historical park, in Boston, includes other sites associated with the Revolutionary War and the birth of the nation, such as Bunker Hill, Faneuil Hall, the Old State House, the Old North Church, and Paul Revere's home, as well as Charlestown Navy Yard, where USS *Constitution*, "Old Ironsides," is berthed. In nearby Lowell, Massachusetts, a unique park named for the town, preserves the industrial heritage of this textile milling center and first planned industrial community in the United States.

Two parks reflect the contributions of maritime industry to American history: the Salem Maritime National Historic Site and the San Francisco Maritime National Historical Park. Salem Maritime National Historic Site in Essex County, Massachusetts, preserves the center of America's first great seaport: Salem. From Salem, Yankee merchants sailed to every corner of the globe, bringing back to New England the trade goods of Europe and the Mediterranean, spices from the Orient, and rawhides from ranches in Mexican California for the growing leather industry of Massachusetts' north shore. Two wharves, once lined with warehouses and shops, now stretch as open expanses of grass and stone into the harbor off the park's shores. The Custom House that stands at their head dates from a time when the federal budget was largely dependent on revenues gained by taxing shipborne imports.

Few people realize that the National Park Service protects the nation's largest collection of historic ships, including two on the East Coast: the World War II destroyer *Cassin Young*, moored close to *Constitution* at Charlestown Navy

Yard, and the lightship No. 116, *Chesapeake*, on loan to the Baltimore Maritime Museum. Seven ships are the primary resource of San Francisco Maritime National Historical Park. The 1886 squarerigger *Balclutha*, with its tall spars and yards, dominates the park's Hyde Street Pier on San Francisco's northern waterfront. The ships include the ferryboat *Eureka*, built in 1891 to carry railroad cars and then rebuilt in 1922 for transbay passenger service; the three-masted lumber schooner *C.A. Thayer*; the flat-bottomed scow schooner *Alma*, an ideal vessel for navigating the shallows and shoals of San Francisco Bay and its tributaries, and the large, wooden-hulled steam schooner *Wapama*. Other vessels are the 1907 steam tug *Hercules* and the 1915 paddlewheel tug *Eppleton Hall*. Nearby, and managed by private groups in cooperation with the National Park Service is *Jeremiah O'Brien*, the last unaltered World War II Liberty Ship. *O'Brien* participated in the D-Day landings. Another wartime vessel, the submarine *Pampanito*, saw extensive combat service in the Pacific.

Ships are not the only maritime resources in the National Park System. Maritime activity, a pervasive thread in the fabric of American history, is reflected by the fifty-nine lighthouses in the park system, including the most famous American light at Cape Hatteras National Seashore. Several parks contain the buildings and facilities of the United States Lifesaving Service, established in 1878 to assist mariners in distress on shipwreck-plagued shores. Demonstrations of lifesaving equipment are popular summer attractions at Cape Hatteras and Cape Cod national seashores. A lesser-known but nationally important facility, the Point Reyes Lifeboat Station, the last operational rail-launching lifeboat station on the Pacific coast, is part of Point Reyes National Seashore in California. Boston National Historical Park includes the previously mentioned Charlestown Navy Yard, with one of the country's oldest drydocks and ropewalks.

Some parks include what might at first glance not even be considered a maritime resource. Moore's Creek National Military Park in Currie,

North Carolina, for example, includes, in addition to the 1776 battlefield, stands of live oak and pitch pine, both the staples of the state's maritime stores industry. Live oak was highly valued for shipbuilding, while pine made turpentine and tar for caulking decks and seams in hull planking. The national park system also contains canals, the most famous unit being the Chesapeake and Ohio Canal National Historical Park, which connects Cumberland, Maryland, and Harpers Ferry, West Virginia, with the District of Columbia and Maryland.

Westward migration is celebrated and its traces preserved in a number of parks, the main one being Jefferson National Expansion Memorial, where the Gateway Arch, a gleaming 630-foot-high stainless steel structure designed by Eero Saarinen, stands on the banks of the Missouri River at St. Louis – the traditional "gateway" to the frontier. An expansive subterranean museum beneath the arch's base commemorates the Westward migration with a series of exhibits.

Another earlier gateway is also included in the system. Cumberland Gap National Historical Park, on the border of three states – Virginia, Tennessee and Kentucky – memorializes the blazing of the wilderness road by Daniel Boone and others who opened an important route for trans-Allegheny migration. Other areas of similar significance include trading posts and forts: Hubbell Trading Post in Arizona, Fort Larned in Kansas, and Bent's Old Fort in Colorado. Sites associated with the late aspects of the Westward movement include Golden Spike National Historic Site, scene of the May 10, 1869, ceremony at Promontory, Utah, where the Union Pacific and Central Pacific railroads met, linking the continent by rail for the first time.

Thirty-two sites, buildings, structures, and monuments in the national park system commemorate seventeen U.S. presidents. Five areas each are accorded to two men: Abraham Lincoln and Theodore Roosevelt. Lincoln's Kentucky birthplace, his Indiana boyhood residence, the Illinois home he left to assume the presidency, Ford's Theater and the adjacent Petersen home – where he was assassinated and died – and the Lincoln Memorial commemorate the sixteenth President. Roosevelt is honored at his birthplace, the site of his inauguration, Sagamore Hill – his home and estate on Long Island, Theodore Roosevelt Island on the Potomac outside Washington, and Theodore Roosevelt National Park. Roosevelt, like Lincoln, is also honored at Mount Rushmore. Other presidential sites in the park system commemorate George Washington, John Adams, Thomas Jefferson, John Quincy Adams, Martin Van Buren, Andrew Johnson, Ulysses S. Grant, James A. Garfield, William Howard Taft, Herbert Hoover, Franklin Delano Roosevelt, Harry S. Truman, Dwight David Eisenhower, John F. Kennedy, Lyndon Baines Johnson, and Jimmy Carter. The only first lady thus honored is Eleanor Roosevelt, whose "Val-Kill" estate at Hyde Park is a national historic site.

One park closely associated with every president since Herbert Hoover is Catoctin Mountain Park in western Maryland. Selected as the site for the official presidential retreat by Franklin Delano Roosevelt in 1942, an isolated camp was established in what was then known as Catoctin Recreational Demonstration Area. A series of cabins were built there between 1936 and 1939 as part of a government project to develop recreational facilities on agriculturally depleted lands. The retreat, named "Shangri-La," was gradually added to and renovated. President Dwight D. Eisenhower, who frequently used the retreat during his administration, renamed it for his grandson, giving the retreat its famous name, "Camp David." In 1954 the government created 6,000-acre Catoctin Mountain Park, which surrounds Camp David, out of the former recreational demonstration area lands. Heavily guarded and closed to the public, Camp David is the scene of important conferences, meetings and decisions of national and international importance. Another site in the national park system associated with the presidents is the White House, the grounds of which are administered by the National Park Service.

Other great Americans are commemorated at

several places in the national park system. Two great men, educator Booker T. Washington and scientist Thomas Alva Edison, are represented by Tuskegee Institute National Historic Site, Alabama, and Thomas Edison National Historic Site in Glenmont, New Jersey. Tuskegee Institute, founded by Booker Washington in 1881, was a major and pioneering institution of higher learning for black Americans. The site incorporates the college buildings, some constructed by the students, "The Oaks" – Booker T. Washington's home–and the George Washington Carver Memorial. Edison National Historical Site includes the laboratories and "Glenmont," the twenty-three-room home, office and library of the great inventor, who spent forty-four years there developing such technological marvels as light bulbs, phonographs and motion pictures.

The humanities are represented by six parks which honor artist Georgia O'Keefe, author Edgar Allen Poe, sculptor Augustus Saint Gaudens, play-wright Eugene O'Neill and poets Henry Wadsworth Longfellow and Carl Sandburg. Poe's Philadelphia residence, a national historic site, is included as part of Independence National Historical Park. Georgia O'Keefe National Historic Site in Abiquiu, New Mexico, commemorates her artistic career at her home and studio. Frederick Douglass' Washington, D.C. home, "Cedar Hill," commemorates the former slave and statesman as Frederick Douglass National Historic Site. The Martin Luther King Jr. National Historic Site in Atlanta, Georgia, preserves the birthplace, boyhood home, church and grave site of the great civil rights leader. The home of Clara Barton, the "Angel of Mercy" and founder of the American Red Cross, is preserved at Clara Barton National Historic Site in Glen Echo, Maryland. The home also served as Red Cross national headquarters from 1897 to 1904. The home of John Muir, the nation's leading proponent for national parks, in Martinez, California, was designated a national historic site in 1964. Another park proponent and prominent landscape architect, Frederic Law Olmsted, is commemorated by a national historic site in Brookline, Massachusetts, that preserves his "Fairstead" estate.

The National Park Service also manages a diverse collection of fortifications that include reconstructed Colonial forts; the well-preserved Castillo de San Marcos – the oldest masonry fort in the continental United States – in St. Augustine, Florida; later brick and granite forts built in the decades preceding the Civil War; turn-of-the-century, reinforced-concrete coastal defense batteries, and Cold War missile bases. Among the more memorable is Fort Jefferson – the largest all-masonry fortification in the Western world – built between 1846-1868 to guard the Florida Straits at the Dry Tortugas. Other important sites are Fort Pulaski – the brick walls of which finally yielded to Union bombardment in 1862, heralding the end of the brick and stone walled forts – and the sixteenth-century military complex at San Juan National Historic Site in Puerto Rico, the oldest fortifications in the territorial limits of the United States.

A collection of different types of concrete seacoast defense batteries at New York and San Francisco harbors, preserved at both Gateway and Golden Gate national recreation areas, are the country's best collection of turn-of-the-century "Endicott" fortifications. Similar fortifications are found at Gulf Islands National Seashore and at some of the earlier masonry forts that were "modernized." Huge concrete batteries tunneled into the coastal hills north of the Golden Gate, mounted sixteen-inch naval guns capable of firing twenty-six miles out to sea. The batteries were built to defend against Japanese attack during the Second World War. Golden Gate National Recreation Area also offers the only Nike missile battery open to the public, with elevating missile platforms, dummy missiles and underground complexes of early atomic technology.

The evolution of the national park idea is evident in the different types of areas, notably the national parkways, national seashores, national preserves, national wild and scenic rivers and national recreation areas. These areas reflect changes as early as the 1930s and as late as the 1970s – years of continued growth in the national park system during which ninety-three new areas were added, most of them historic sites. The additions were made partly because of increased visitation in the extant national parks, resulting ultimately in the creation of thirteen new recreation areas. Visitor figures had increased from twenty-one million in 1941 to thirty-three million in 1950 and seventy-two million in 1960. Fourteen natural parks were added between 1933 and 1964, among them the well-known Grand Teton, Channel Islands, Everglades, Big Bend and Capitol Reef. Major changes in the park concept were also introduced, in the most radical rethinking to the national park system since the inclusion of the historical areas.

The first parkway, authorized in 1928, was the Mount Vernon Memorial Highway, later expanded into the George Washington Memorial Parkway. Others followed, springing up around Washington, D.C. A change occurred in 1933 and 1934 when the Blue Ridge and Natchez Trace parkways were authorized as Depression-inspired public works projects. These parkways established protected roadways that allowed motorists expansive scenic vistas. The Blue Ridge Parkway, for example, stretches 469 miles along the Appalachian Mountains of Virginia and North Carolina. The overlooks, historic sites, craft demonstrations and souvenir shops on this, the longest scenic drive in the world, can only have encouraged the American cult of the automobile. The Blue Ridge Parkway is certainly one of the most traversed of the scenic routes. John D. Rockefeller Jr. Memorial Parkway in Wyoming links Grand Teton and Yellowstone national parks and was named in honor of this philanthropist who purchased lands for several parks, notably the land covered by Grand Teton. Natchez Trace Parkway follows the historic Natchez Trace, a major trail linking the nation to the old Southwest through Tennessee, Missisippi and Alabama. Despite the popularity of the parkways, the consequent intrusion of cars into wilderness areas was to be fought vigorously after World War II by a number of groups and influential citizens wanting a return to the old park concept. No new parkways have been built in recent decades, nor indeed have there been any extensions to ones already in existence.

The idea of national park areas as enclaves of public recreation was further developed and another new type of protected area, the national seashore, was introduced after a seashore recreation survey in 1934. Americans resident on the coasts flocked to the ocean for recreation in record numbers during the late nineteenth and early twentieth centuries. Consequently, the National Park Service recommended that twelve unspoiled stretches of Atlantic and Gulf Coast beaches be added to the National Park System. The first was Cape Hatteras National Seashore, authorized in 1937. The lands of the slowly acquired national seashores now include seventy miles of barrier island beaches on Bodie, Hatteras and Ocracoke islands. South of Hatteras is Cape Lookout National Seashore, stretching fifty-eight miles along Portsmouth Island, Core Banks and the Shackleford Banks. Established in 1966, Cape Lookout is accessible only by private boat or ferry. Eight other seashores and four national lakeshores on the Great Lakes: Pictured Rocks, Apostle Islands, Indiana Dunes and Sleeping Bear Dunes, are now part of the national park system. They include two Gulf Coast seashores: Gulf Islands and Padre Island. Gulf Islands embraces a 150-mile stretch of offshore islands, keys, beaches and marshes in Mississippi, Alabama and Florida. In Texas, Padre Island National Seashore protects a 113-mile-long barrier island. Point Reyes National Seashore, north of San Francisco, covers 67,265 acres of the vast Point Reyes Peninsula and its cliff-lined beaches in Drakes Bay, as well as the prominent, rocky headland of Point Reyes and a ten-mile sweep of its sand dune-lined beaches. In New England, Cape Cod National Seashore, authorized in 1961, incorporates forty miles of beaches and marshes managed in partnership with the Fish and Wildlife Service, the Commonwealth of Massachussetts and private property owners.

The national seashores and lakeshores, originally planned as destinations for people seeking aquatic recreation, gradually came to be recognized as unique habitats for wildlife and as unspoiled wildernesses in their own right. A belated appreciation of natural resources led to battles to keep the National Park Service from developing these areas to meet the requirements of such forms of public recreation. At Point Reyes National Seashore, for example, plans to build paved roads and beachside public facilities on unspoiled Limantour Spit were defeated. The national seashores, while providing recreational opportunities, now place their emphasis on maintaining scenic, natural and cultural values. Many incorporate significant historical and archaeological resources. For example, the shores of Cape Hatteras, the "Graveyard of the Atlantic," are littered with the battered remnants of wooden vessels lost off its shores. Shifting sands frequently uncover the bones of lost ships on the beach, often in sight of the lighthouses that were built to guide mariners past this dangerous reach of coast.

As the precepts of conservation and ecology became more firmly entrenched in the 1960s and 1970s, new areas were added to the national park system to protect rivers and wildlife. The Wild and Scenic Rivers Act of 1968 authorized the inclusion of rivers with "outstandingly remarkable scenic, recreational, geologic, fish and wildlife, historic, cultural or other similar values ..." in the national park system. There are currently nine wild and scenic rivers in the national park system and 119 affiliated wild and scenic rivers not in the system.

The need for parks to preserve wilderness land was not the main drive behind the creation of the first national parks – even Yellowstone only incidentally incorporated and protected wilderness areas within boundaries drawn largely to take in scenic wonders. The passage of the Wilderness Act in 1964 designated six million acres of federal lands, for the most part national forests, as wilderness areas. The act also required the National Park Service to study park lands in order to assess their suitability for inclusion in the National Wilderness Preservation System. Many parks are now included in this system which stresses the retention of areas of "primeval character and influence, without permanent improvement or human habitation" in which there were to be no permanent roads, no commercial enterprises,

no landing of aircraft nor overflights at altitudes lower than 4,000 feet, no motor vehicles, motorized equipment or motorboats, nor any structure or installation. The greatest addition to the system came on December 2, 1980, when President Jimmy Carter signed the Alaska National Interest Lands Conservation Act. In all, 47,080,730 acres were added to the national park system, converting Alaska's national monuments into national parks or preserves and adding substantial new lands. For example, Mount McKinley National Park became part of Denali National Park and Preserve, adding to the old park four million acres of wildlife habitats and the southern flanks of the mountain. Other monuments which were substantially augmented and changed included Gates of the Arctic, Katmai, Noatak, Glacier Bay, Wrangell-St. Elias, the Bering Land Bridge, Lake Clark and Kenai Fjords.

At the time the Wilderness Act passed in 1964, the National Park Service, in response to the increased demand for public recreation facilities, formally adopted recreation as a principle of the National Park System. This, in addition to encouraging recreational development in existing parks, eventually produced eighteen national recreation areas. Nearly all are centered on or near water, with many located around man-made lakes and reservoirs, such as Lake Mead near Las Vegas, Nevada, Amistad Reservoir in Texas and Franklin Delano Roosevelt Lake in Washington – created by Coulee Dam.

Two bold departures from the traditional role of the National Park Service were tagged with the "recreation area" label when they were created in 1972. As the result of a campaign by former Secretary of the Interior Walter Hickel, who sought to bring "parks to the people," two areas were established in major urban centers: New York and San Francisco. Rather than try to attract inner-city dwellers, particularly the disadvantaged, to more isolated wilderness parks, the National Park Service and Congress instead created these two areas out of nationally significant, natural, cultural and scenic areas in the two cities. Accordingly, Gateway and Golden Gate national recreation areas were established in October 1972 and since then both have grown. Golden Gate grew the fastest to become one of the most popular units in the national park system. Golden Gate, or GGNRA as it is also known, attracts more than twenty million visitors annually. The park's success is in large measure due to its accessibility and the matchless resources within it, among them views of the Golden Gate and the Pacific Ocean, a notorious former federal penitentiary on Alcatraz Island, a major cultural center at Fort Mason, wilderness areas in Marin and San Mateo counties, sixty miles of shoreline and more than 2,000 historic buildings, sites and structures. It was recently designated as an international biosphere. Golden Gate contains more individual National Register of Historic Places and National Landmark designated properties than any other unit in the system. The Golden Gate's designation as a national recreation area is in some ways misleading – it is to all intents and purposes a national park.

At the end of the twentieth century attention was focused once again on the basic role of national parks. The fundamental challenge of the vying needs of recreation and public access balanced with the need to protect and conserve natural and cultural resources. Ecologist Aldo Leopold observed in 1938: "Recreational development is not the job of building roads into lovely country, but of building receptivity into the still unlovely human mind." Recreation in this sense implies a re-creation of the human spirit in order that it may view the wilderness as a living organism and see mankind's dependence upon the environment for survival. "Civilization has so cluttered this elemental man-earth relation ... that awareness of it is growing dim. We fancy that industry supports us, forgetting what supports industry." The creation of parks for the protection of endangered wilderness was hampered by a failure to include in the proposal an adequate peripheral area to protect the main resource – as was the case, for instance, when reclamation projects in the surrounding area of the Everglades drained off water vital to the protected marshes. A naturalist described the Everglades as "a waterless hell under a blazing sun" in 1961. Elsewhere protected

wildlife roams out beyond the artificial, politically created park boundaries and onto lands where they can be hunted, and loggers clear cut trees right up to park boundaries.

Clearly parks need to be bigger and must be able to take into account the complexity and scope of natural interrelationships. The world is a living organism – as the problems of rain forest destruction are now showing – and parks in the future may not only be essential means of reinforcing human perceptions of the natural world – they may help save it.

However, parks are being "loved to death" as visitation levels continue to rise and the unabated popularity of the automobile brings more and more people. Some historic homes which were built only to handle the original resident family and its guests are being beaten apart by the pounding of millions of feet. The problem involves a Catch-22 situation: the need to preserve parks for future generations by engendering public support through providing for more visitors who, by sheer force of their numbers, are battering their heritage. J. Horace McFarland, President of the American Civic Association and strong supporter of the nation's parks, noted in 1934: "In the matter of the National Park development I am bound to say that we must accept compromises if assaults on the parks from the selfish citizens, of whom we have not a few, are to be repelled." The problem, as old as the national parks themselves, may in time pass as cultural maturity develops in our society and the concept of preservation as a higher goal than simple profit, takes firmer hold. As the population grows, it will inevitably result in some of the parks being accessible only to a fortunate few unless more parks are created and a different standard of park enjoyment is adopted that does not stress a hurried, drive-by approach to the national park experience.

Meanwhile external threats of development continue to plague the parks – not only the wilderness parks with their mineral, hydroelectric or timber assets, but also those parks in urban areas, particularly the historic sites, where urban and suburban growth hems their borders or takes over surrounding lands that should have been included in the parks but were not. A national campaign was waged in 1989 to stop a shopping mall and adjacent homes from being built on land located just outside a Civil War historic park, but which had nonetheless also been bathed in the blood of Civil War soldiers. The land in question was eventually included in the park, but its acquisition was triggered by acrimony, anguish and bitter debate, and was finally accomplished at prohibitive cost.

The rate of creation of national parks has slowed in recent years. Since 1980 only a handful of new areas have been created as part of a deliberate policy of the government. The pressing needs of the existing parks, understaffed and underfunded, gave rise to a determination to find money with which to address critical needs, namely to restore and rehabilitate park resources. While this was a sound policy for the many parks already in existence, the resultant lack of new acquisitions or expansions to protect critical habitats, historical and archaeological resources or scenic vistas has allowed incomparable resources to slip away in the frenetic pace of modern development. More parks are needed of course, parks that would encompass the diversity of the existing political system and embrace new concepts of partnership of park authorities with state, local governments and private citizens. Such a partnership should not mean a lesser standard of environmental care, but rather a commitment to protect and preserve significant resources as if they were federally owned.

Recent initiatives have expanded the role and the mission of the National Park Service. Heritage trails, which link areas in the national park system with state parks, monuments and memorials, as well as hitherto unrecognized local landmarks or resources, are one such initiative. In New Jersey, a heritage trail along the coast, without necessitating acquisition of new land by the National Park Service, is in the planning stages that involve the National Park Service as a facilitator and interpreter. This experiment should not only bolster tourism but also encourage a higher degree preservation and protection of the cultural, natural, scenic

and recreational resources identified on the trail. A countywide partnership, inspired by Salem Maritime National Historic Site in Essex County, Massachusetts, seeks a similar result for historical resources associated with Colonial settlement, maritime trade and the leather and textile industries.

Fresh examination of the existing parks also highlighted the necessity to open a new frontier and create national parks underwater. The national park system now controls more than 2,250,000 acres of submerged land, an acreage equal to the size of Yellowstone National Park – but divided into eighty separate areas. Well-known examples include Channel Islands, Isle Royale and Virgin Islands national parks, as well as Cape Hatteras, Cape Cod and Point Reyes national seashores. Most submerged park land, however, is found in lesser known areas, such as parks on rivers, or smaller lakes.

Sport diving is increasing in the United States. More than three million people are certified divers and each year thousands more learn. New technology and undersea discoveries are opening up the undersea world at the same time. Just as the natural, cultural, scenic and recreational value of the parks on land led to greater efforts toward preservation and public attention and enjoyment, so the same happened with those parks underwater. Coral formations and reef life in the Virgin Islands or at Biscayne National Park, and the rich marine life found in the submerged kelp forests of Channel Islands National Park are as compelling as wilderness areas ashore. Another great attraction is the hundreds, perhaps thousands of shipwrecks that lie in the parks.

The national park system protects the remains of various Spanish pataches, fregatas and galleons lost during the sixteenth or seventeenth centuries. Revolutionary War transports and warships scuttled by the defeated British lie at the bottom of York River off Yorktown in Colonial National Historical Park. The battered iron and steel hulls of square-riggers wrecked in the late nineteenth century lie under the waters of Cape Cod and Point Reyes national seashores, Golden Gate National Recreation Area and Fort Jefferson

National Monument. Two important ships lie wrecked in an area which is under consideration to be incorporated in War in the Pacific National Historical Park in Guam. In Apra Harbor, the German raider *Cormoran*, which was interned in the harbor and scuttled by its crew in April 1917 when the United States entered World War I, is nudged by the wreck of the Japanese armed transport *Tokai Maru*, sunk by American submarines during World War II. No other place in the world is known to offer visitors the opportunity to rest one hand on the remains of a ship lost in "the war to end all wars" and the other on a ship sunk in the war that followed.

At Isle Royale National Park the wrecks of ten ships, representing a fifty-year span of Great Lakes shipping history, lie beneath the cold waters of Lake Superior. Remarkably well preserved, these wrecks are sunken ghost towns compelling exploration. Some wrecks are accessible by foot as well as by water. Close to the Utah border, on the banks of the Colorado River at Lees Ferry in Glen Canyon National Recreation Area, lies *Charles H. Spencer*, a stern-wheeler built, disassembled and rebuilt during 1913 in the Arizona desert, only to be abandoned within a few months. These and other wrecks as well as the fascinating undersea world of marine life are exciting aspects of the marine parks.

With the imminence of the twenty-first century, the National Park Service and the national park system find themselves facing many of the same problems and challenges that led to the original creation of the parks and the agency. Perceptions of what the parks both should and what they should not be abound. As Barry Mackintosh has noted, the growth of the park system provided the nation with a symbol of its ideals; the diversity and growth of the parks, as well as the limitations of and egregious damage to some parks, has demonstrated both the strengths and weaknesses of the political process. Yet, as Mackintosh stated, "the wonder is not that the System has fallen short of the ideals set for it, but that it has come so close." Fear of developing the parks to their detriment, and an insufficient appreciation of parks as islands of the natural world are fading. The park concept will prevail due to the soundness of setting aside places where the natural world is maintained and protected and where historic sites and structures allow visitors interaction with the past and an understanding of our heritage.

Previous page: Bass Harbor Head Lighthouse, Acadia National Park, a welcoming sentinel to mariners traveling the dangerous Atlantic Ocean coastline. One of America's smaller parks, Acadia preserves a stretch of Maine's rugged shoreline (right), which is made up of chiseled, granite cliffs, jagged rocks and tiny inlets.

Facing page: Virginia's Shenandoah National Park, comprised of forest-clad slopes interspersed by flower-covered meadows, with the Blue Ridge Mountains seen in the distance as a bluish haze. Above: the dramatic and weirdly shaped Mammoth Onyx Cave, one of many underground limestone caverns found in Mammoth Cave National Park. Once home to Indian tribes, these subterranean passages and chambers, still not totally explored, are a popular Kentucky attraction.

Right: a panoramic view looking across the Great Smoky Mountains. Often thought to be the oldest continuously inhabited area of the country, it was home to the Cherokee Indians for some thousand years. Overleaf: Roaring Fork, near Grotto Falls, one of many cascading streams in this park, which is situated on the Tennessee/North Carolina border.

The prehistoric-looking Everglades National Park is made up of dense mangrove swamps (right), towering cypress trees and rich subtropical vegetation, sustained by a shallow river that flows from Lake Okeechobee to Florida Bay. Nearby drainage and industrial activity threatened the park's delicate ecosystem, but preservation schemes have saved this semi-acquatic environment and its endangered wildlife. A young alligator (above) basks in the Florida sun – once hunted for its skin, this reptile has now become a common Everglades sight. Top: a Little Blue Heron, one of many bird species in the park. Overleaf: the Corkscrew Swamp boardwalk, overhung with Spanish moss.

Both Biscayne National Park, at the south-east tip of the Florida peninsula, and Virgin Islands, off the Florida coast, possess stunning underwater scenery, the fascinating colors and textures of their coral reefs attracting countless visitors. Virgin Islands National Park covers three-quarters of the island of St. John, and is an unspoilt tropical paradise of brilliant white sandy beaches, sparkling coves and richly forested mountains, as found at famous Trunk Bay (right), on the island's northwest coast.

Hot Springs National Park, Arkansas, is an interesting combination of undisturbed woodlands and therapeutic, thermal waters. The rocky hills surrounding the busy resort of Hot Springs possess extensive hiking trails and are covered with dense forests and vivid wildflowers, such as the dogwood on West Mountain (above). Facing page: the distinctive twin towers of the color-washed Arlington Hotel, seen from Bathhouse Row, one of the buildings to benefit from the government-supervised bathhouses opened to take advantage of the waters of the hot springs.

Voyageurs, Minnesota's first national park, boasts attractive forested lake countryside, which includes this island in Lake Kabetogama (top), strikingly silhouetted against an evening sky. Canoes were once the main means of transport for early explorers and missionaries crossing these lakes and streams, and one of the attractions available to visitors today is to join the Voyageur Canoe *on Rainy Lake (above). Facing page: Isle Royale, the largest island in Lake Superior, was designated a national park in 1931. With its prolific conifers and hardwood trees, this lake-bound wilderness shelters many different species of animal and wildflower.*

North Dakota is home to Theodore Roosevelt National Park (above), and South Dakota to Badlands National Park (top and facing page). Strangely sculpted shapes, ancient fossils and colorful rock strata are typical of both preserves, the harsh landscape of each being formed by water cutting through the soft layers of rock. South Dakota also contains Wind Cave National Park, situated in the Black Hills, and renowned for its underground caverns and fine fossils.

Tranquil waters overlooked by dramatic peaks are a feature of the unspoiled splendor of Rocky Mountain National Park, Colorado. The most spectacular section of this range is contained within the park, and includes more than one hundred peaks that are over 11,000 feet in height. Right: Flat Top Mountain forms an impressive backdrop to picturesque Dream Lake.

Fall-colored aspens (above) with their silvery trunks (facing page top), and the deep blue of Bear Lake (facing page bottom), framed with green and yellow, are typical of the rich color and beauty evident in the Rocky Mountains. The flora and fauna are strictly protected in this wildlife sanctuary and many nature lovers are attracted by the fine variety of species to be found here.

Square Tower House (right), Navajo Canyon, and Cliff Palace (overleaf), with some two hundred rooms, are among the incredible cave dwellings in Colorado's Mesa Verde National Park. Built on cliff ledges by Indians who had moved from the mesa tops during the 12th century – probably for defensive reasons – these homes were then abandoned a century later, leaving them very much as they are today.

47

The stark grandeur of Big Bend National Park, Texas, is well illustrated by Santa Elena Canyon (above), an immense limestone gorge cut by the mighty Rio Grande. In this park rugged outcrops rise above arid plains (facing page top), dotted with sparse greenery and colorful desert blooms, as at Sotol Vista Overlook (overleaf). Facing page bottom: the colorful "Window from the Basin." Surprisingly, this inhospitable terrain sustains over one thousand different kinds of plant, and more than two hundred different species of bird have been observed here.

Looming above the desert of Guadalupe Mountains National Park, Texas, stands the fortress-like bulk of El Capitan (above), once part of a barrier reef created when this area was covered by a shallow inland sea. Facing page: beneath the rugged foothills of this range, and formed over millions of years, Carlsbad Caverns National Park, New Mexico, is an underground wonderland of giant chambers filled with rock formations of every imaginable shape, color and size. Delicate forms tinted by minerals, contrast with massive stalactites and stalagmites.

Above: the beautiful cone-shaped Blue Mesa, with its colorful bands that mark ancient layers of marsh, is part of Arizona's Petrified Forest National Park. Facing page: the tree trunks (top) sparkle with silica, iron and manganese oxides and these petrified logs (bottom), some two hundred million years old, are scattered across the arid, brilliantly colored plains. Over the years the slow process of petrification has gradually replaced the wood tissues with mineral deposits until these incredible "stone trees" no longer feel like wood to the touch.

One of the more impressive and most-visited of the United States' natural wonders is Arizona's Grand Canyon. Overlooks on both sides of the gorge offer breathtaking views across an immense area of multicolored rock formations that were created by the combined effects of the Colorado River, land upheavals and climatic and chemical erosive forces. A mile deep and some two hundred miles long, this remarkable canyon was established as a national park in 1919.

Numerous vantage points, accessible by road, provide exceptional views over the intricately sculpted peaks and buttresses of the Grand Canyon, giving some idea of the magnitude and grandeur of this national park. Mohave Point on West Drive (facing page), and Yaki Point (top and overleaf), are among the lookouts situated on the canyon's rim. Above: sparse vegetation clings precariously to the red rock layers and sheer walls of the Grand Canyon.

The Sentinel (left), a massive sandstone outcrop, towers above the waters of the North Fork of the Virgin River in Zion Canyon. This multicolored gorge is the main focus of Utah's Zion National Park, and was created mainly by the gradual cutting action of the Virgin River. Within ten miles of the Utah-Nevada border is Great Basin, another national park, which encompasses a large area containing numerous peaks and caves.

Bryce Canyon National Park (these pages) is made up of striking, brilliantly colored rock
sculptures, columns and towers, as seen along Queen's Garden Trail (top) and from Paria View
(facing page). Named after Ebenezer Bryce, a Scottish immigrant and Morman settler to the area,
and authorized as a national park in 1924, this forbidding terrain is home to a surprising variety
of wildlife. Overleaf: a magnificent panorama of shapes and colors seen from Inspiration Point.

Utah's Capitol Reef National Park (these pages) is larger than Bryce Canyon and Zion combined, yet, being more inaccessible, is less well known. Water, in the form of rivers, glaciers and rain, has played a major part in creating the wonders found here, and the slow process of erosion that has carved shapes that include those in Capitol Gorge (facing page top), Cassidy Arch (facing page bottom) and Eph Hanks Tower (above), continues imperceptibly to alter their forms.

Above: the spectacular Needles area at the southern end of Canyonlands National Park, where weathering and jointing have created orange-red and white banded spires (facing page top). Island in the Sky (facing page bottom), which rises above the stark terrain, has been carved away by the Green River on the west and the Colorado River on the east. Overleaf: the red-hued Wooden Shoe, with delicate white peppergrass flowers in the foreground.

Arches National Park lies on the Colorado Plateau, Utah, an area once covered by an inland sea. Over millions of years, erosion of the sandstone has resulted in remarkable geological wonders that include South Park Avenue (above), made up of monumental vertical slabs up to three hundred feet high. The park contains more than two hundred arches – among these are the immense span of North Window (top) through which Turret Arch can be seen, Delicate Arch (facing page), and the massive, buttress-like, sandstone arcs of Double Arch (overleaf).

Jackson Lake (right), surrounded by dense coniferous forests and overlooked by the blue-gray Teton Mountains, is the largest body of water in the area and is typical of the scenery to be found in Grand Teton National Park. Wyoming's 13,747-foot-high Grand Teton peak (overleaf) dominates the Snake River Valley, a fertile area of lush green spruce, pine and fir.

Yellowstone, America's oldest national park, is a strange and spectacular world of hot springs, geysers and other thermal features. These include powerful Castle Geyser (top), Upper Geyser Basin, surrounded by a massive cone of gray geyserite. Facing page: Black Sand Basin is remarkable for its Emerald Pool, which has a translucent center fringed by vivid orange-yellow algae. In contrast are the twisted outlines of nearby trees (above). Overleaf: the Firehole River.

Glacier National Park, Montana, was established in 1910 to preserve over one million acres of magnificent Rocky Mountain wilderness. Two Medicine Lake (top) with Mount Sinopah in the background, and Swiftcurrent Lake (above) with Grinnel Point and Mount Gould beyond its shores, are examples of the sparkling lakes, fed by glacial meltwater and waterfalls, that are very much part of the beauty of this area. Dramatic Fusillade Mountain (facing page) and the imposing face of Garden Wall (overleaf), which overlooks McDonald Creek, are typical of the park's rugged scenery.

Washington's North Cascades National Park, often referred to as the "American Alps," encompasses wild and unexplored mountainous countryside. The formidable Mount Shuksan, part of the mighty Cascades Range, dominates the park and overlooks the peaceful waters of Picture Lake (left and overleaf).

Olympic National Park, Washington, boasts some beautiful and varied attractions that include glaciers, rain forests, wildflower-covered meadows and small lakes. Above: the magnificent Hall of Mosses, on the upper Hoh River, an area of ancient, gnarled trees covered with vivid green mosses. Facing page: tranquil Lake Crescent, framed with daisies, the largest body of water in the park, and (overleaf) boats skimming the surface of Big Bend, Hood Canal, off Olympic Peninsula.

Above: the leafy Grove of the Patriarchs and (facing page) Falls Creek, Mount Rainier National Park, Washington. Overleaf: the snow-capped summit of Mount Rainier, the highest peak in the Cascade Range, is seen in the distance across lupine meadows. This volcanic mountain and its complex glacier system are popular with nature lovers, hikers and mountain climbers.

Left: the cone of Wizard Island rises from the incredible blue waters of Crater Lake, Oregon. The lake is contained within a caldera, formed some ten thousand years ago when the volcanic Mount Mazama erupted and collapsed in on itself. At 1,932 feet, Crater is the deepest lake in the United States and the focal point of this park.

Full of grandeur and dignity, the magnificent redwoods, the world's tallest trees, soar above the forest floor in California's Redwood National Park. Above: a striking view of Ladybird Johnson Grove, with a moss-covered sapling outlined in golden light, and in contrast, a mist-shrouded forest scene in Del Norte Coast Redwoods State Park (overleaf). Off the Pacific coast is Channel Islands National Park, also in California, an area rich in both marine mammals and seabirds.

Lassen Volcanic, California's smallest national park, is known for its volcanic origins and hydrothermal activity. Among its most visited features is the moon-like landscape of the hot spring basin, Bumpass Hell (right). Contrasting with this area is richly colored Manzanita Lake (overleaf), edged with pines and firs and over-looked by dramatic Lassen Peak. Rising high above the park the mountain erupted regularly between 1914 and 1915, resulting in widespread destruction of the forest-clad northeastern slopes.

Dominated by the Sierra Nevada mountains, Yosemite National Park is an area of grandeur and beauty. Granite walls, towering sequoias, canyons, rivers and waterfalls are all typical of the splendid park scenery, as can be seen in Yosemite Valley (left), with Bridalveil Falls to the left of the picture, and Dewey Point in the center. Overleaf: a spectacular vista from Tunnel View, the sheer, gray bulk of El Capitan facing the massive rounded Cathedral Rocks across the forested, glacier-carved valley.

Sequoia National Park is home to majestic and ancient sequoias that include the famed General Grant (facing page), estimated to be between 2,000 and 2,500 years old. Related to the redwood tree, sequoias are one of the largest species in trunk size. Above: the formidable peaks of the Sierra Nevada dominate Kings Canyon National Park and overlook the tumbling waters of the Roaring River.

These pages: the unspoiled wilderness of four of southern Alaska's breathtaking, yet desolate, national parks. Top: Katmai, known as "Valley of Ten Thousand Smokes," features the still waters of a lake formed when Mount Katmai collapsed during the volcanic eruption of Novarupta, in 1912. Above: a killer whale cruises through Aialik Bay, Kenai Fjords National Park. Facing page: blue-white Riggs Glacier (top), one of many rivers of ice in Glacier Bay National Park, and within Wrangell-St. Elias National Park, majestic Mount Drum looms above Willow Lake (bottom).

Northern Alaska is home to the diverse wildernesses of forest-covered Kobuk Valley (facing page) and Gates of the Arctic national parks. Further south is Denali National Park (top), dominated by the towering mass of Mount McKinley, at 20,320 feet North America's highest mountain. Above: Lake Clark National Park, renowned for its beauty and the variety of its spectacular scenery.

Left: Devastation Trail, Kilauea Crater, on Hawaii or "Big Island," the largest in the chain of Hawaiian islands. Molten lava still bubbles beneath the surface of Kilauea Volcano, one of the active cones enclosed in Hawaii Volcanoes National Park, and a major tourist attraction. Legend has it that the periodic eruptions are a result of angering the goddess Pele.

Above: Hawaii's Halemaumau Crater. Also within the Hawaiian archipelego is Haleakala National Park, established on the island of Maui in order to preserve the spectacular Haleakala Crater (top). Named "House of the Sun" by the Hawaiians, after a legend where the demigod Maui captured the sun in order to make it promise to travel more slowly across the sky each day, this volcano is now dormant. Facing page and overleaf: the lush paradise of the National Park of Samoa, renowned for its dense tropical rainforest, rugged coral reefs and sparkling white beaches.

INDEX